STONEHENGE

Published and Distributed by:
Lemonade Books
www.lemonadebooks.com
U.S.A.

ISBN 0-9766834-0-7

Printed in the U.S.A.
First Printing April 2005

Scientists believe that thousands of years ago, an ancient people lived on the plains of England. They think that this people looked to the stars for all the answers. These astronomers built a magnificent structure that could record and predict how the universe would act. This structure is now known as Stonehenge, but what if the real reason for Stonehenge was a little different...

Through the dim moonlight and flickering shadows of the fire, the eager children awaited their Grandfather's story. The story about a circle of rocks known as Stonehenge.

Grandfather loved to share his stories. He began, "before the cold winds blew and the white snow covered the sleeping land, the ancient villagers mounted their trusty saber toothed friend in search for food."

As they peered out from behind their cover, they spied a strange herd in the distant valley.

Before their eyes, standing ten times the height of any other, was a giant mammoth.

"Can you imagine all the steaks and roasts and hamburgers we could get from that mammoth? It could feed us through the whole winter," said one of the villagers.

"But if we get the mammoth, how will we cook it? It is much too big for our campfires," one of the villagers said.

An oven was suggested, but they decided that even with all their strength, they would not be able to shut the door.

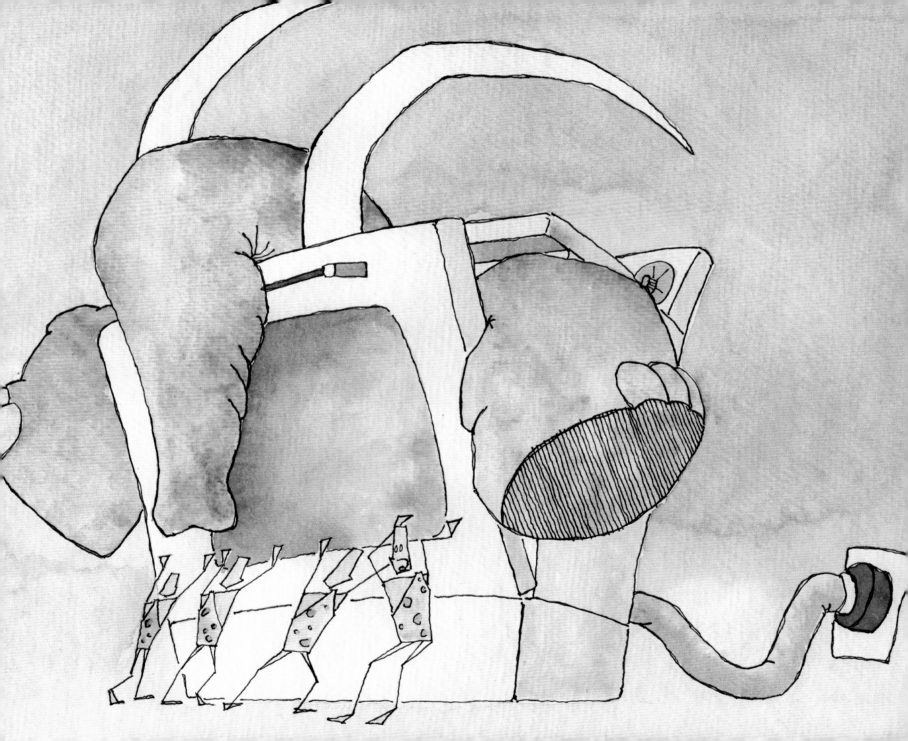

"We could cook the mammoth in a pot and add our secret sauce?" But they decided it would boil over.

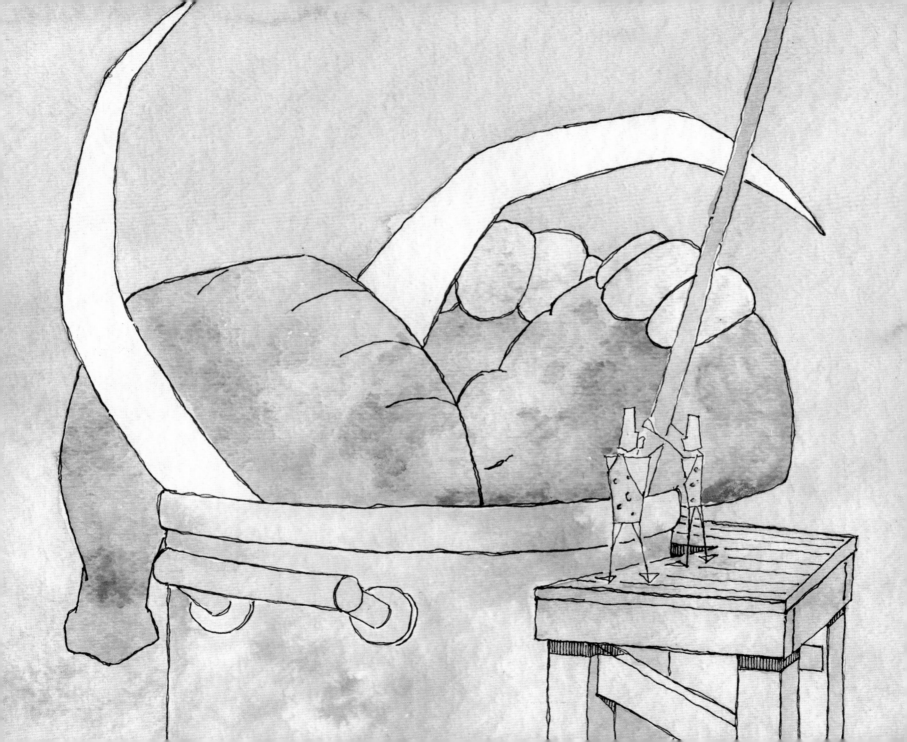

"We could roast it on a spit," said another. But it was decided that the fires wouldn't be big enough.

A toaster was suggested, but quickly rejected.

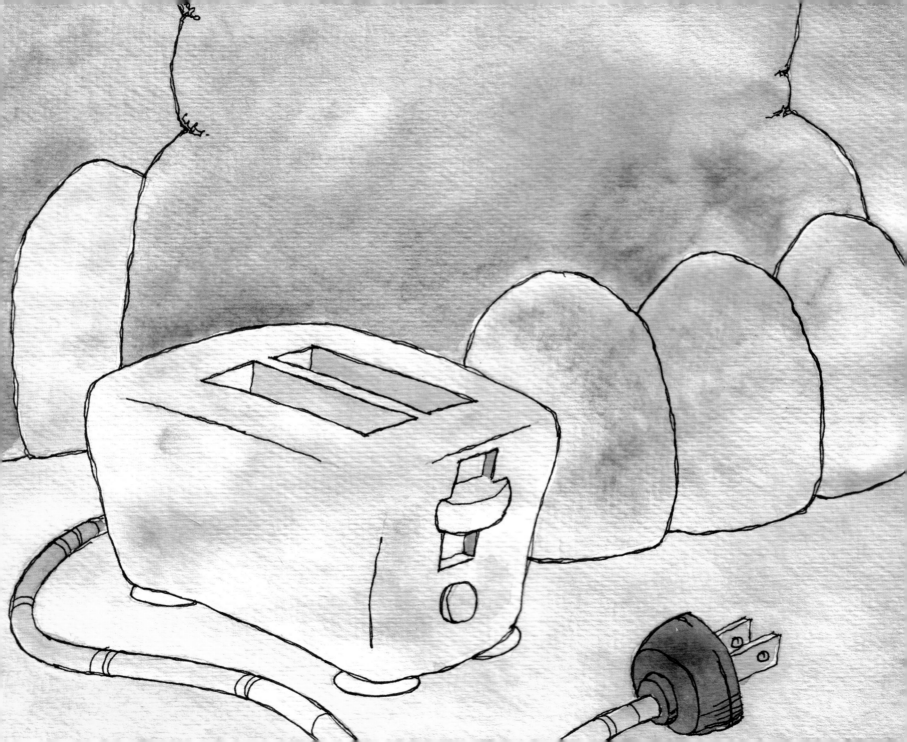

"I've got it. We could build a giant grill big enough for the mammoth!" The villagers loved the idea. Their mouths began to water just thinking of the barbecue ahead.

The villagers traveled miles and miles away to find stones large enough.

They pulled and lifted and dragged and tugged as they built...

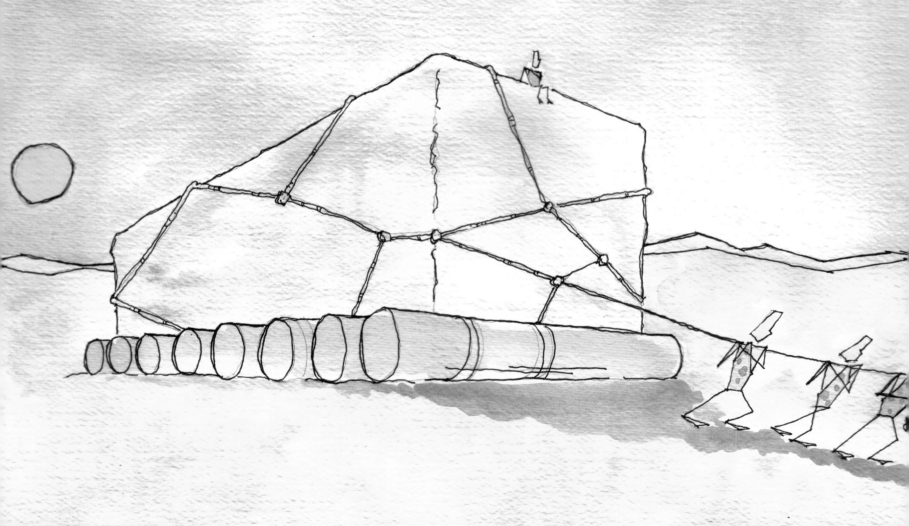

. . . and built . . .

. . . and built . . .

...Until it was finished. The villagers stared up in awe at the finished grill.

It didn't take the villagers long to get their mammoth. What a feast!

No giant mammoths were ever seen again so the grill went unused year after year, until it finally fell apart. So the rocks stand waiting…